Battle at Sea

DESTROYERS

AVERY LEE

BLACK RABBIT BOOKS

Bolt is published by Black Rabbit Books
P.O. Box 227, Mankato, Minnesota, 56002.
www.blackrabbitbooks.com

Alissa Thielges, editor
Jason Knudson, designer

Library of Congress Cataloging-in-Publication Data
Names: Lee, Avery author
Title: Destroyers / Avery Lee.
Description: Mankato, MN: Black Rabbit Books, [2027] | Series: Battle at sea | Includes bibliographical references and index. | Audience: Ages 8-12 | Audience: Grades 4-6
Identifiers: LCCN 2025055130 (print) | LCCN 2025055131 (ebook) | ISBN 9781645826279 library binding | ISBN 9781645828419 paperback | ISBN 9781645826330 ebook
Subjects: LCSH: Destroyers (Warships)—United States—Juvenile literature | CYAC: Destroyers (Warships) | Warships | LCGFT: Instructional and educational works
Classification: LCC V825.3 .L44 2027 (print) | LCC V825.3 (ebook) | DDC 623.825/4--dc23/eng/20260126
LC record available at https://lccn.loc.gov/2025055130

Printed in India

Image Credits

Black Rabbit Books/Jason Knudson 14, 19, 23; DVIDS/Petty Officer 1st Class Fred Gray IV, 11 (t), Petty Officer 2nd Class Elliot Schaudt, 24–25; Freepik/andriistepaniuk, 26, Brgfx, 9, macrovector, 9; Shutterstock/TebNad, 32; Wikimedia Commons/DENNIS GRIGGS/U.S. Navy, cover, Don S. Montgomery, USN (Ret.), 14, MC1 Woody Shag Paschall/U.S. Navy, 16–17, National Museum of the U.S. Navy, 18–19, National Museum of the U.S. Navy, 20–21, Petty Officer 1st Class Michelle Turner, 12–13, United States Navy/Huntington Ingalls Industries, 4–5, U.S. Navy/John F. Williams, 22–23, U.S. Navy/Mass Communication Specialist Seaman Chelsy Alamina, 1, 31, U.S. Navy/Mass Communication Specialist Seaman Michael Starkey, 3, 11 (b), U.S. Navy/Mass Communication Specialist 3rd Class Jonathan Sunderman, 6–7, U.S. Navy photo by Petty Officer 2nd Class Nicholas Russell, 9, U.S. Navy photo by Photographer's Mate 3rd Class Ryan Jackson, 29; Every effort has been made to contact copyright holders for material reproduced in this book. Any omissions will be rectified in subsequent printings if notice is given to the publisher.

CONTENTS

CHAPTER 1

Ready to DEFEND

A destroyer sails fast. It zig-zags across the open sea. Its big **radar** scans the skies, looking for danger. Suddenly, an alarm goes off. An enemy has sent a **missile**. And it is heading toward the ship!

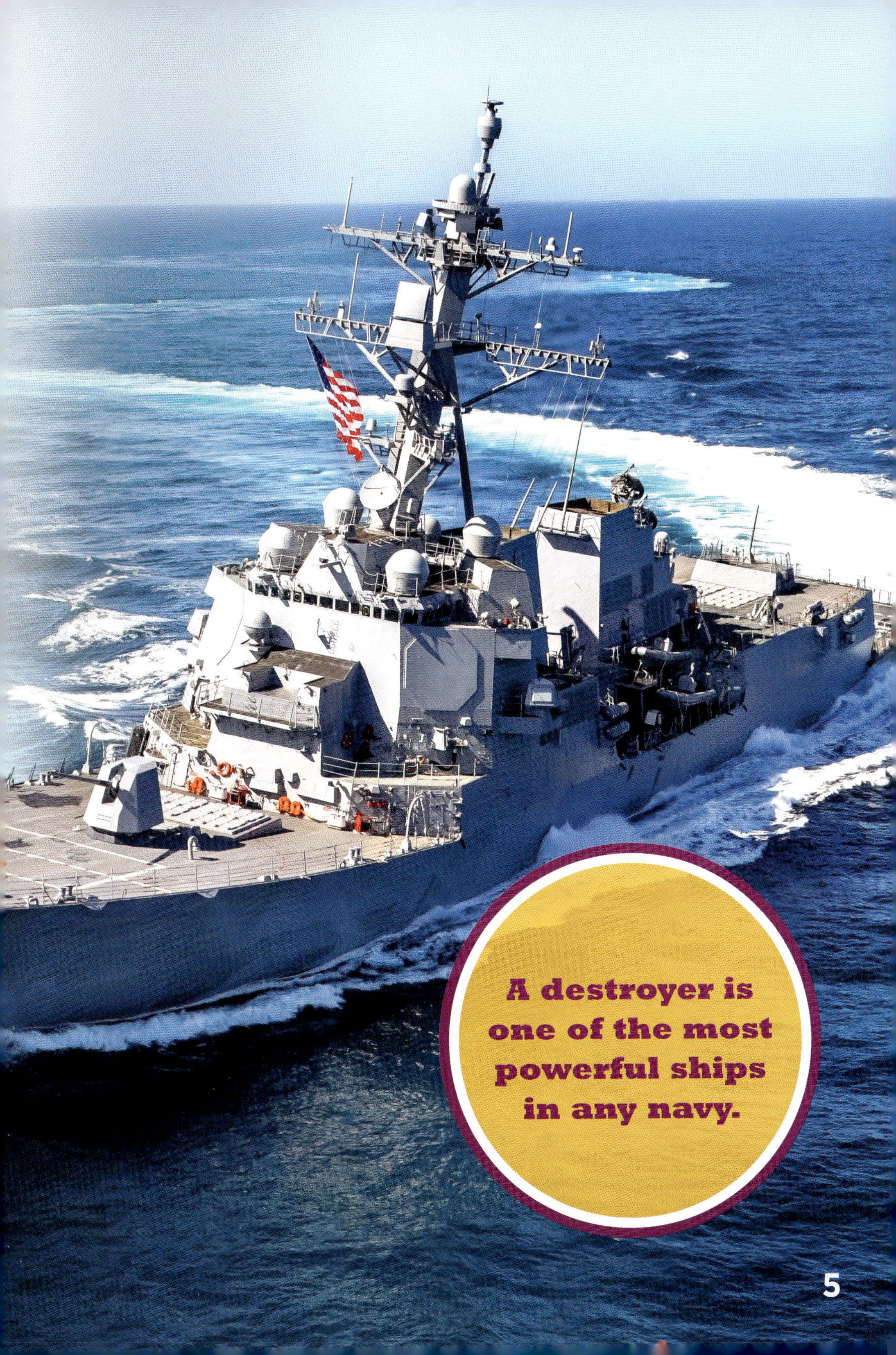

A destroyer is one of the most powerful ships in any navy.

Strike in Seconds

The crew moves quickly. They have less than a minute to respond. The weapon systems unlock. The ship prepares to fire back.

Soon, a missile roars into the sky. It curves toward the threat. Moments later—BOOM! The weapons hit each other. They blow up in the air. The **fleet** is safe again.

CHAPTER 2

Ship BODYGUARD

A destroyer is a powerful warship. The U.S. Navy uses them to **escort** larger ships. In a fleet, usually two of them guard an aircraft carrier. They are joined by cruisers and a submarine. Together, they form a shield. If danger is spotted, a destroyer can attack fast.

POSSIBLE DANGERS

Small but Mighty

Most destroyers are smaller than cruisers or carriers. But they are quick. They are also packed with smart technology. Tools jam signals. Enemies can't find U.S. ships.

When attacked, every second counts. High-tech computers control the ship's weapons. They help make quick decisions.

These ships also carry helicopters.

PARTS OF A DESTROYER

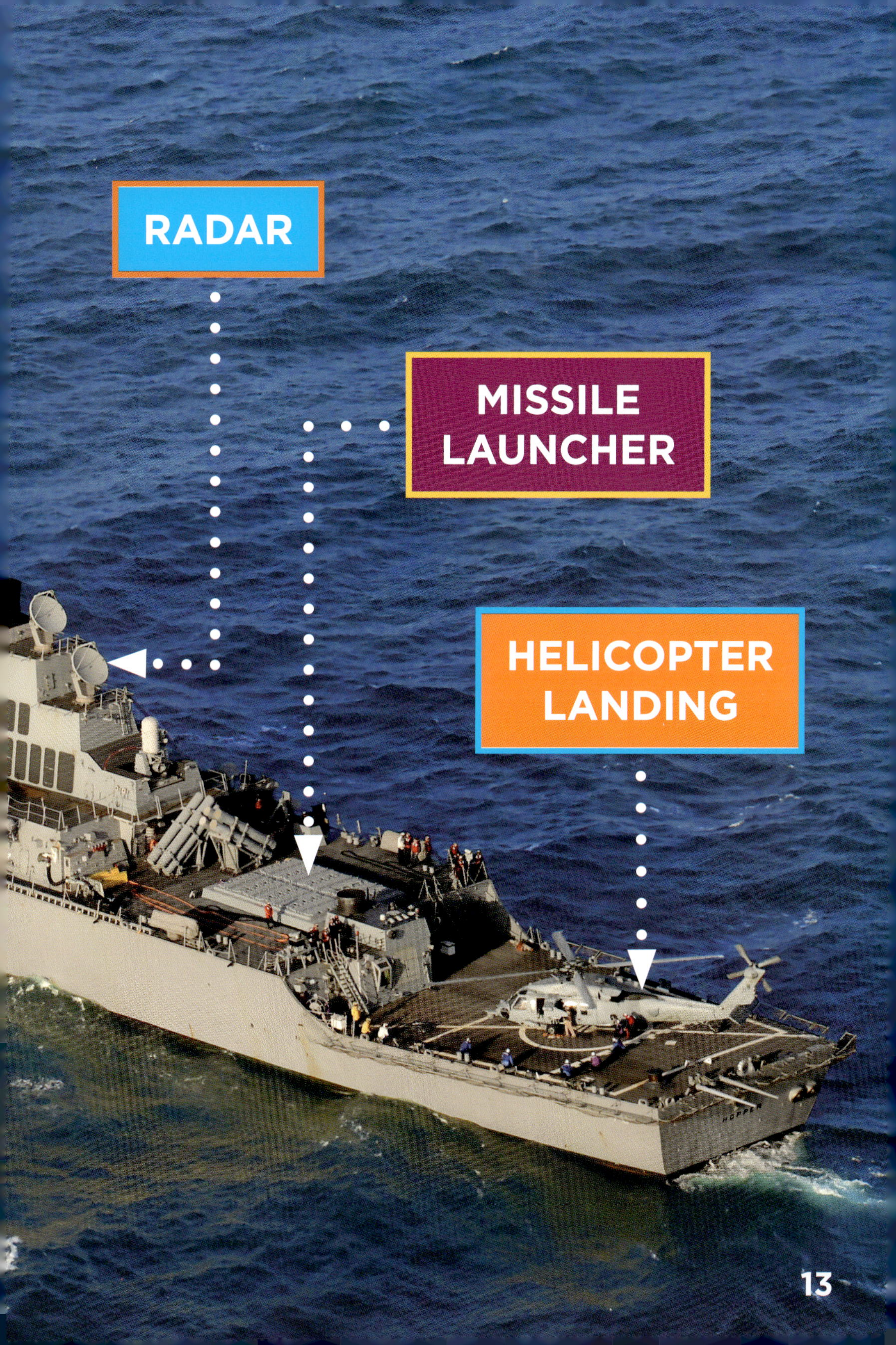
RADAR
MISSILE LAUNCHER
HELICOPTER LANDING

ABOVE WATER
missiles
surface ships
RADAR
SONAR
submarines
torpedoes
BELOW WATER

Searching Sky and Sea

Destroyers have big radars like SPY-1 or SPY-6. They track enemies far away. The SPY-3 can track air and surface objects at the same time. **Sonar** listens deep underwater. It searches for submarines. If found, the ship fires a **torpedo**. Destroyers are ready for all kinds of attacks.

Projecting Power

Destroyers can attack enemies on land, too. They carry Tomahawk missiles. They can hit places 1,000 miles (1,609 kilometers) away. This offers support for battles that are far from the ocean. Their presence alone sends a message of strength. Each ship is a show of power.

Big guns fire at other ships and enemies on land.

CHAPTER 3

Types of DESTROYERS

The U.S. Navy uses two classes of destroyers. The Arleigh Burke is an older class. The ships are the **backbone** of the navy. Many are still in use. The Zumwalt class is newer. It is much bigger. It has newer technology and weapon systems.

COMPARING *LENGTHS*

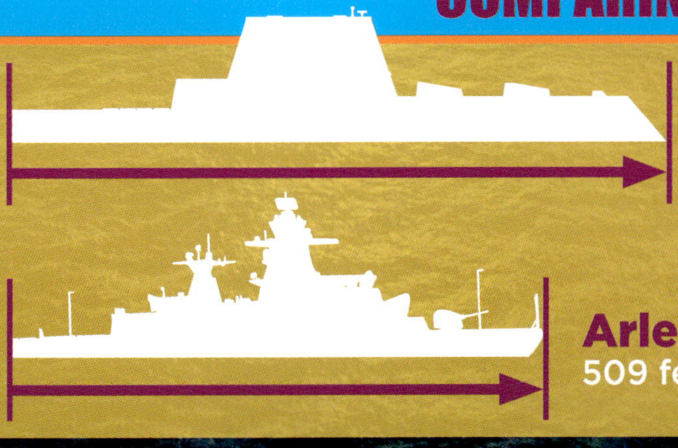

Zumwalt
610 feet (186 meters)

Arleigh Burke
509 feet (155 m)

Sneaky Design

The Zumwalt class looks much different from the Arleigh Burke class. Its sides lean in like a triangle. It has smooth, flat surfaces and sharp angles. This shape helps it hide from enemies. The Zumwalt is much bigger, too. It uses electric power. The ship runs quieter this way.

Most warships are painted gray. They blend in with the ocean and sky.

Future Class

A new class may be ready in the 2030s. It is being designed for future danger. It will have laser weapons and a better radar. It may carry a **hypersonic** missile. This powerful weapon has a rocket booster. It can blast into space. It travels at Mach 5+. That is five times the speed of sound!

SUPER *SPEEDS*

HYPERSONIC WEAPON	MACH 5
CRUISE MISSILE	MACH 4
SR-71 BLACKBIRD	MACH 3
F-16 FIGHTING FALCON	MACH 2
F-35 LIGHTNING II	MACH 1

CHAPTER 4

On MISSION

Destroyers watch over busy sea lanes. They guard sea-to-land ships and supply ships. The ships have also helped during rescues. They may deliver supplies after big storms. Destroyers sail all over the world. They can operate almost anywhere.

U.S. NAVY MAJOR BASES

EUROPE
ASIA
AFRICA
AUSTRALIA
Manama, Bahrain
Yokosuka, Japan
Sasebo, Japan

Support at Sea

Destroyers are built for high speed and sharp turns. They strike, move, and reload rapidly. If there is an emergency, the Navy can send this ship right away. Destroyers protect people and aid **allies**. They keep the seas safe for the U.S. Navy.

GLOSSARY

ally (AL-ahy)—a country that supports and helps another country

backbone (BAK-bohn)—the most important or strongest part of something

escort (ES-kawrt)—to go with someone or something to give protection or guidance

fleet (FLEET)—a group of military ships controlled by one leader

hypersonic (HAHY-per-son-ik)—traveling at a speed of more than five times the speed of sound

missile (MIS-uhl)—a rocket-powered weapon used for distant targets

radar (RAY-dar)—a device that sends out radio waves for finding the location and speed of a moving object

sonar (SOH-nar)—a device that uses sound waves to find objects underwater

torpedo (tawr-PEE-doh)—a bomb shaped like a tube that is fired underwater

LEARN MORE

BOOKS

Hamilton, John. *United States Navy*. Minneapolis: Abdo Publishing, 2021.

Koestler-Grack, Rachel A. *Curious about Destroyers*. Mankato, MN: Amicus Learning, 2025.

West, David. *Warships*. New York: Crabtree Publishing Company, 2020.

WEBSITES

Destroyer Facts for Kids

kids.kiddle.co/Destroyer

Navy

kids.britannica.com/kids/article/navy/353522

INDEX